Oceanside Public Library
330 N. Coast Highway
Oceanside, CA 92054

PIANO • VOCAL • GUITAR

SHOW BOAT

Applications for performance of this work, whether legitimate, stock, amateur, or foreign, should be addressed to:

RODGERS AND HAMMERSTEIN THEATRE LIBRARY
229 West 28th Street, 11th Floor
New York, NY 10001
Telephone: (800) 400-8160
Facsimile: (212) 268-1245
Email: theatre@rnh.com
Website: www.rnh.com

Photography by Catherine Ashmore and Martha Swope

ISBN 0-7935-4553-6

For all works contained herein:
Unauthorized copying, arranging, adapting, recording or public performance is an infringement of copyright.
Infringers are liable under the law.

HAL•LEONARD®
CORPORATION
7777 W. BLUEMOUND RD. P.O. BOX 13819 MILWAUKEE, WI 53213

Visit Hal Leonard Online at
www.halleonard.com

CIVIC CENTER

LIVENT (U.S.) Inc.
presents

SHOW BOAT

starring

JOHN McMARTIN   ELAINE STRITCH
REBECCA LUKER   MARK JACOBY

and

LONETTE McKEE
as "Julie"

Music by   Book and Lyrics by
JEROME KERN   OSCAR HAMMERSTEIN II

Based on the novel "Show Boat" by **EDNA FERBER**

featuring

JOEL BLUM   DOROTHY STANLEY
GRETHA BOSTON   DOUG LaBRECQUE

with

MICHEL BELL
as "Joe

TAMMY AMERSON   DAVID BRYANT   JACK DABDOUB
LORRAINE FOREMAN   MIKE O'CARROLL
SHEILA SMITH   RALPH WILLIAMS

Production Design by   Costumes Designed by   Lighting Design by   Sound Design by
EUGENE LEE   FLORENCE KLOTZ   RICHARD PILBROW   MARTIN LEVAN

Production Musical Supervisor   Orchestrations by   Dance Music Arranged by
JEFFREY HUARD   ROBERT RUSSELL BENNETT   DAVID KRANE
and WILLIAM DAVID BROHN

Assistant to Mr. Prince
RUTH MITCHELL

Choreographed by
SUSAN STROMAN

Directed by
HAROLD PRINCE

LIVENT (U.S.) Inc. is a subsidiary of Live Entertainment of Canada Inc.

GERSHWIN THEATRE

First Performance at this Theatre – September 22, 1994

ALL PRODUCTION PHOTOS ARE OF THE ORIGINAL CAST

NOV 1 5 2007

3 1232 00815 0379

The Arrival Of The Cotton Blossom

The Story

Elaine Strich as Parthy

Rebecca Luker as Magnolia
To the right: Mark Jacoby as Gaylord Ra—

Dawn on the levee at Natchez on the Mississippi River, 1887. While children play and black stevedores and women work, white townsfolk gather to greet the arrival of Cap'n Andy's floating theatre (Cotton Blossom). A parade begins, and Cap'n Andy introduces the members of the "Show Boat" Troupe: his wife, Parthy; the song-and-dance team Ellie May Chipley and Frank Schultz; the romantic leads — Stephen Baker and his wife, Julie LaVerne. He encourages everyone to attend that evening's show and concert (Cap'n Andy's Ballyhoo). Tension grows between Pete, the Cotton Blossom's engineer, and Steve caused by Pete's efforts to win Julie's affection by giving her unwelcome gifts. Steve warns Pete to keep away from his wife. Cap'n Andy insists that the "Show Boat" Troupe is "one big happy family." Steve strikes Pete. When Pete threatens revenge, Cap'n Andy fires him.

Shortly after, Gaylord Ravenal, a riverboat gambler, is drawn to the Cotton Blossom by the sound of a piano being played on board. He discovers the player is Cap'n Andy's young daughter, Magnolia, and is immediately attracted to her (Make Believe). The Sheriff appears and warns Ravenal that he cannot stay in Natchez longer than twenty-four hours because he was charged with killing a man. Ravenal protests, saying he proved the murder was in self-defense. The Sheriff says he must leave before nightfall. Joe, who is in charge of mooring the Cotton Blossom in each town it visits, notices the growing attraction between Magnolia and Ravenal. He thinks about life on the Mississippi (Ol' Man River).

Parthy disapproves of Julie giving Magnolia piano lessons and doesn't want the performer to be friends with her daughter. Despite her wishes, Magnolia and Julie meet in Queenie's kitchen pantry on the Cotton Blossom and chat about the stranger Magnolia has just met. They are soon joined by Joe and the stevedores and women (Can't Help Lovin' Dat Man).

At a nearby riverfront saloon, Ravenal tries his luck at cards and loses (Till Good Luck Comes My Way). Pete informs Frank he is going to tell the Sheriff that Julie is of racially mixed parentage and is passing herself off as a white woman. In Mississippi, miscegenation — intermarriage between races — is a crime.

In the Cotton Blossom's auditorium, Queenie, Joe, the stevedores and the women are cleaning and polishing. Queenie senses that something terrible is about to happen (Mis'ry's Comin' Aroun'). Cap'n Andy, Parthy, Steve, Julie and Magnolia arrive to rehearse that night's show, "The Parson's Bride." Ellie runs in and interrupts the rehearsal, telling Steve that the Sheriff and Pete are on their way to arrest him and Julie. Steve whips out a large pocket knife and, reassuring Julie, cuts her finger and drinks her blood. The Sheriff arrives, accompanied by Pete, and announces that the Cotton Blossom has a case of miscegenation on board. Steve asks whether the Sheriff would consider a white man to be white if he had "negro blood" in him. The Sheriff replies "one drop of negro blood makes you a negro in these parts." Steve claims he has "more than a drop of negro blood in me." Windy, the Cotton Blossom's pilot, supports Steve's statement. The Sheriff backs down, but forbids Cap'n Andy from giving the show that night. Despite Magnolia's protests, Julie and Steve pack their belongings and leave the Cotton Blossom.

Lower middle: "Can't Help Lovin' Dat Man," with (L-R) Lonette McKee as Julie (behind Magnolia), Rebecca Luker as Magnolia, Michel Bell as Joe, Gretha Boston as Queenie (kneeling) and the Show Boat ensemble.

Far right: Rebecca Luker as Magnolia (top) and Mark Jacoby as Ravenal (bottom)

Cap'n Andy realizes he needs a new leading man and lady. Frank arrives with Ravenal, who seeks passage on the Cotton Blossom. Cap'n Andy grants his request by pressing him into service as the leading man. Despite Parthy's objections, Cap'n Andy makes Magnolia the new leading lady. Soon, the on-stage romancing becomes real as their love grows (I Have the Room Above Her).

The next night, on the levee at Fort Adams, Ellie is hawking tickets to that night's show when she is approached by some star-struck fans (Life Upon the Wicked Stage). Parthy and Cap'n Andy bicker. Parthy tells him that she does not approve of Ravenal and his affection for Magnolia. Cap'n Andy defends Ravenal. Meanwhile, ticket sales for the balcony, where the black people must sit, are slow. Queenie volunteers to help sell the balcony seats (Queenie's Ballyhoo).

Inside the now sold-out auditorium, the performance of "The Parson's Bride" begins. Frank enters, portraying the villain, and threatens Miss Lucy, played by Magnolia. A backwoodsman, who is carried away by the story, stands up, and rebukes Frank. He draws a pistol, and then fires a shot at him. The show boat audience panics as Frank runs out of the auditorium and Magnolia and Ravenal flee the stage. The performance comes to a halt. Cap'n Andy calms everyone and acts out the remainder of the play as a one-man show to depict what everybody would have seen.

Later that night, Ravenal and Magnolia meet on the top deck of the Cotton Blossom. Ravenal asks her to marry him. They proclaim their love for each other (You Are Love).

The next morning, on the levee in Natchez, the townspeople gather to celebrate Magnolia and Ravenal's wedding (Act One Finale - The Wedding Celebration).

<hr/>

ACT TWO

The levee at Natchez, 1889. During a thunderstorm, Magnolia and Ravenal's daughter, Kim, is born. Parthy sings a lullaby to her granddaughter (Why Do I Love You?). Ravenal reveals he has struck it rich gambling, and tells Magnolia that they are moving north to Chicago (Montage One). The Ravenals continue to prosper through Gaylord's gambling as four years pass until it's the Chicago World's Fair of 1893 (The Sports of Gay Chicago).

In Natchez, Cap'n Andy reads a letter to Parthy from Magnolia and Ravenal. Parthy becomes suspicious that all is not well with them. Cap'n Andy suggests that they travel to Chicago to visit their granddaughter. Back in Chicago, Ravenal's luck has ended. He, Magnolia and Kim, now a young girl, are evicted from the Palmer House Hotel.

Top: Lonette McKee as Julie

Bottom: (L-R) Gretha Boston as Queenie and Michel Bell as Joe

Chicago, 1899. Frank and Ellie, have become a successful vaudeville team and are about to open at the Trocadero Night Club. They are searching for lodgings. While inspecting an apartment room in a second class boarding house, they are surprised to learn the tenant is Magnolia. A letter arrives from Ravenal. He has decided to leave Magnolia and Kim, believing they will be better off without him, and suggests that Magnolia should return to her parents on the show boat. Magnolia refuses to return to that life. Frank offers to help Magnolia get a job at the Trocadero Night Club.

Top: "The Parson's Bride," with (L-R) Rebecca Luker as Magnolia, Mark Jacoby as Ravenal (on stage), and Mike O'Carroll as Backwoodsman, Elaine Stritch as Parthy (in box).

Bottom: "Looking Out To Sea," with (L-R) Joel Blum as Frank and Dorothy Stanley as Ellie.

At St. Agatha's Convent where Kim is a student, Ravenal visits his daughter (Alma Redemptoris Mater). He tells her he is going away on a business trip, then disappears. At the Trocadero Night Club, Julie — who was forced to leave the show boat years earlier — is now working as the featured singer. Drinking from a small flask she carries in her purse, she reminisces about Steve, who abandoned her. She rehearses a new song for her act (Bill), then goes to her dressing room. Frank and Magnolia arrive. Frank arranges for Magnolia to audition. As Magnolia sings (Can't Help Lovin' Dat Man — Reprise), Julie walks in, sees her and realizes how much her old friend needs a job. Julie leaves. The doorman enters and says that Julie has left. Magnolia is hired to replace Julie.

The next night, New Year's Eve, 1899. Cap'n Andy and Parthy arrive at the Palmer House Hotel to discover that Ravenal, Magnolia and Kim are gone. Cap'n Andy thinks they are out celebrating and asks Parthy to go with him to look for them. She decides to stay at the hotel. Cap'n Andy meets two young ladies and goes with them to the Trocadero Night Club. Frank and Ellie entertain the crowd (Goodbye, My Lady Love). Magnolia takes to the stage and begins to sing (After the Ball). The audience, which came to hear Julie, jeers her. Recognizing his daughter on stage, Cap'n Andy stands up, encourages her and persuades the crowd to listen to her. Magnolia finishes her act in a blaze of glory.

Twenty-one years pass. Magnolia becomes a famous musical comedy star. Fashions change as headlines proclaim the events of the day, including the assassination of the Archduke Ferdinand in Sarajevo, the outbreak of World War I and Armistice. Julie begs on the street. Black street entertainers perform the songs of the day including the new musical style — jazz. They perform a new dance — the Charleston (Montage II — Ol' Man River).

The levee at Natchez, 1927. The era of gaslight is over and the show boat is now lit with electric lights. Cap'n Andy, who had written a letter to Ravenal inviting him to visit, tells Gaylord that he has sent a telegram to Magnolia asking her to come home.

Top: John McMartin as Cap'n Andy (center) performs with the Show Boat ensemble.
Lower: Tammy Amerson as Kim (dancing on car) and the Show Boat ensemble.

Ravenal is hesitant about seeing his ex-wife again or his daughter, Kim, now a young woman and a Broadway star in her own right.

The next night, Magnolia and Kim have arrived. Kim entertains with a sample from her Broadway repertoire (Kim's Charleston). An old woman appears who witnessed Magnolia and Ravenal's marriage, and tells them how happy she is that they are still together. Reunited, Magnolia and Ravenal realize how deep and everlasting their love remains (Act Two Finale).

Dennis Kucherawy

MAKE BELIEVE

Lyrics by OSCAR HAMMERSTEIN II
Music by JEROME KERN

The game of ___ "just sup - pos - ing" ___ is the
sweet - est ___ game I know. ___ Our ___ dreams are
more ___ ro - man - tic than the world we see.

Copyright © 1927 UNIVERSAL - POLYGRAM INTERNATIONAL PUBLISHING, INC.
Copyright Renewed
All Rights Reserved   Used by Permission

OL' MAN RIVER

Lyrics by OSCAR HAMMERSTEIN II
Music by JEROME KERN

Copyright © 1927 UNIVERSAL - POLYGRAM INTERNATIONAL PUBLISHING, INC.
Copyright Renewed
All Rights Reserved   Used by Permission

CAN'T HELP LOVIN' DAT MAN

Lyrics by OSCAR HAMMERSTEIN II
Music by JEROME KERN

Copyright © 1927 UNIVERSAL - POLYGRAM INTERNATIONAL PUBLISHING, INC.
Copyright Renewed
All Rights Reserved   Used by Permission

MIS'RY'S COMIN' AROUN'

Lyrics by OSCAR HAMMERSTEIN II
Music by JEROME KERN

Copyright © 1928 UNIVERSAL - POLYGRAM INTERNATIONAL PUBLISHING, INC.
Copyright Renewed
All Rights Reserved   Used by Permission

I HAVE THE ROOM ABOVE

Lyrics by OSCAR HAMMERSTEIN II
Music by JEROME KERN

(1st verse tacet)
I have the room a-bove her. She does-n't know I

Copyright © 1936 UNIVERSAL - POLYGRAM INTERNATIONAL PUBLISHING, INC.
Copyright Renewed
All Rights Reserved   Used by Permission

LIFE UPON THE WICKED STAGE

Moderately

Lyrics by OSCAR HAMMERSTEIN II
Music by JEROME KERN

Copyright © 1927, 1928 UNIVERSAL - POLYGRAM INTERNATIONAL PUBLISHING, INC.
Copyright Renewed
All Rights Reserved   Used by Permission

YOU ARE LOVE

Lyrics by OSCAR HAMMERSTEIN II
Music by JEROME KERN

Once a wan-d'ring ne'er-do-well, just a va-grant rov-ing fel-low, I went my way. Life was just a joke to tell, like a lone-ly Pun-chi-

Copyright © 1928 UNIVERSAL - POLYGRAM INTERNATIONAL PUBLISHING, INC.
Copyright Renewed
All Rights Reserved   Used by Permission

WHY DO I LOVE YOU?

Lyrics by OSCAR HAMMERSTEIN II
Music by JEROME KERN

Copyright © 1927 UNIVERSAL - POLYGRAM INTERNATIONAL PUBLISHING, INC.
Copyright Renewed
All Rights Reserved   Used by Permission

BILL

Music by JEROME KERN
Words by P.G. WODEHOUSE
and OSCAR HAMMERSTEIN II

Copyright © 1927 UNIVERSAL - POLYGRAM INTERNATIONAL PUBLISHING, INC.
Copyright Renewed
All Rights Reserved   Used by Permission